D1879780

GOSPEL OF THE GITA

Owing to the antiquity and rarity of this book, certain pages are regrettably absent, and readability is compromised due to the blurring of the original text. If you possess any insights regarding the availability of these missing sections, kindly inform us. Your assistance is crucial in ensuring the completion of this significant work for the benefit of future generations.

GOSPEL OF THE GITA

T. V. KAPALI SASTRY

GYAN

Published by

Gyan Publishing House
5, Ansari Road
Daryaganj, New Delhi-110002
Phone: 011-47034999, 9811692060
E-mail: books@gyanbooks.com

Distribution Network
gyanbooks.com
India, USA, Canada, UK, Australia

© Publisher

All rights reserved. No part of this work may be reproduced, stored, adapted, or transmitted in any form or by any means, electronic, mechanical, photocopying, micro-filming, recording or otherwise, or translated in any language, without the prior written permission of the copyright owner and the publisher.

ISBN: 978-93-6280-392-4 (HB)
First Published, 1960

2nd Impression 2024

Printed at: Gyan Press, Delhi.

The book is sold subject to the condition that it shall not, by way of trade or otherwise, be lent, resold, hired out, or otherwise circulated without the prior publisher's written consent.

GOSPEL OF THE GITA
Author: T. V. KAPALI SASTRY

GOSPEL OF THE GITA

T. V. KAPALI SASTRY

PUBLISHERS' NOTE

An attempt has been made in this volume to bring the contents of the Bhagavad Gita within the reach and understanding of all.

Many relevant problems of popular interest have been discussed and the author has kept in view a comprehensive spiritual background, extending from the Vedas and the Upanishads to modern thought in the field of religion and philosophy. The reader will find in it a complete freedom from sectarian prejudices or interpretations; the scholar will notice points not touched by the authorities in vogue; and the spiritual aspirant is sure to find in it a helpful companion of rare value.

CONTENTS

GOSPEL OF THE GITA

ITS UNIQUE GREATNESS

The Bhagavad Gita is a part of the Mahabhārata which was narrated to King Janamejaya by Vaishampayana, a pupil of Krishnaḍvaipāyana Vyasa who wrote the epic. We have it on the authority of the epic itself that at one time it contained twenty-four thousand verses and was called the Bhārata: later were incorporated into the body of the work Ākhyānas and Upākhyānas, historical legends, vedic parables, allegorical narratives and stories of ethical and religious value handed down by tradition from an unknown past. Thus we have the great compilation, Mahabhārata Samhita, comprising a hundred thousand verses excluding the supplement of Harivamsha. We are not here concerned with the conjectures of the date of compilation of this most voluminous mass of epic literature in the world. It is sufficient for our purpose to note that, unlike the Ākhyānas and Upākhyānas that are separate blocks unconnected with the main story of the great epic, the Bhagavad Gita forms an integral part of the Bhārata war itself. It is not that the story of the war as a historical narrative will be incomplete without a place for the Gita in the Bhishma Parva, but the significance of the wisdom taught in it will be missed if we ignore the battlefield and Arjuna's refusal to fight at the eleventh hour. The import of the Gita's teachings, the spirit of its theme, will escape us if we ignore the occasion that gave rise to its teachings, even though in themselves they are capable of universal application without reference to the battle of Kurukshetra.

Indeed, the Gita embodies in itself the essential teachings of the Upanishads; but not content with a statement of certain spiritual truths, it proceeds to mark out methods of their application in life in a rare manner that distinguishes it from other scriptures. In it we find at every turn a large, free and flexible spirit, a sympathetic understanding of the views in vogue and a sifting of whatever is of permanent and higher value in the crude notions, customary rites and religious beliefs and conventions, of the social order. We also find in it a free place for the extreme philosophic views that counted at the time and a mass of metaphysical ideas that stimulate to a degree the stress and power of thinking; and in a marvellous manner it finds use for all these in its exposition of spiritual truths, in the practical turn it gives, in the profound principles and methods of the one Yoga it has in view for practice and realisation in life. It gives a fresh impetus to old principles and truths, uses old and current words with extended connotation and when these are found insufficient for its purposes, occasionally resorts to new phrasings.

The student of the Gita is familiar with the wide sense it gives to terms like Dharma, Karma, Yajna, Sankhya, and Yoga—which have undergone a magical transformation under the spell of its treatment and are re-born as it were into a vast, rational, philosophic and spiritual sphere from their currency in the local and temporal and scholastic confines of conventional and ritualistic rigidity. It treats of them in an extraordinarily plastic and catholic sense and while recognising the accepted senses and current notions associated with these, it hastens to vivify them into a fresh spirit capable of wider application and far reaching results. Its manner of condemning the aggressive ritualist, *vedavādarata*, or of recovering for us the four-fold type of man as the sense and deeper significance of the social order, by the saving phrase of *guṇa-karma-vibhāgaśaḥ**, is enough to convince us that it rejects what it could not accept and accepts what it could not reject.

The singular and surpassing strength of the Gita lies in its comprehensive outlook and understanding of different types and temperaments; of the higher ideals and truths into which all men are not equally awakened and yet into which it is inevitable all have to grow; of the clash of interests and duties devolving upon man in his attempt to maintain a harmonious relation between his own higher interests and ideals on the one hand and the stern realities of life on the other, between his interests and those of others, between his part as a member of the family and as a member of society or as a member of society and as a creature of the creator. Tolerance and charity are brought home to us when it lays bare the many tangles and conditions of the universally imperfect human

*Character and profession forming the principle of caste division.

nature and the unavoidable conflict in the ways of Dharma, in the law varying with conditions of time, place and occasion, in the not infrequent perplexity in life's battle confronting man, at once a domestic and ethical entity, a human soul and a spiritual being, with an unknown future ahead leaving a dim past behind.

Centuries have elapsed and the Gita has worn well. Its greatness and title to be looked to as an authoritative scripture were recognised long before the Achāryas, and their Bhāshyas on it confirmed its position as one of the three authorities of Vedanta, **Prasthānatraya*, upon which stand the three orthodox schools of later Hindu philosophy.

---

*The Upanishads, the Brahmasutras and the Bhagavad Gita.

THE CRISIS, THE OCCASION

The skies over the battle-field of Kurukshetra were resounding with the echoes of the signal sounds of conches and war-trumpets voicing the preparedness on both the sides of the contending forces. Shri Krishna and Arjuna station themselves in the war-chariot and blow their conches. Everything is ready, the flight of missiles is to begin. Arjuna beholds the army on the enemy's side, when at his request his Divine charioteer stays the chariot between the two armies. He has to give battle to the forces arrayed against him on the side of the wicked cousin. He has to take up arms against Drona, the Acharya who taught him the use of weapons; against Bhishma, the venerable grandsire; against his kinsmen, cousins, brothers and benefactors. He sees and is suddenly sad, moved to self-pity. Struck with horror, his limbs fail him, his mouth is parched. The whole body shivers, his hair stands erect, the skin burns, the weapon slips, his head reels. He finds evil forebodings too. He is sure that no good could result from the killing of his kinsmen. He finds it impossible to think of kingdom at the cost of the lives of these, his teachers, fathers, friends, sons and relatives.

Nor is this a passing emotion, a sentimental wave. He sees great sin too in fighting and slaying the enemy though he be wicked and guilty of betrayal of friendship and of destroying domestic virtues and family ties. That the malicious Duryodhana persists in such a wrong course of action is no excuse for Arjuna to commit the very crime of which he accuses him.

Again he is oppressed by a sense of the serious consequences of the man-slaughter, this crime against humanity. How would it affect society? Would it not lead to lawlessness and social disorder and the wiping out of holy family traditions, religious rites and sacred customs and place the Kuladharma and Varnadharma in danger? Aye, the confusion and corruption accompanying and following a war of that kind could not but leave the sublime ideals of sex-purity and chastity offended, and disturb conjugal and communal relations and duties governed by dharma, when the very fabric of society is sure to be shaken to its foundations.

Thus, in the first outburst of feelings, choked up with emotion, Arjuna sums up his objections to fight, in the words 'Dharma in danger,' and dropping down his bow and arrows he pitifully exclaims: "Ah, how we are resolved upon committing a crime of this magnitude! It is all greed for pleasure. Unarmed I prefer being killed by these my kinsmen armed, who are misguided and over-powered by greed."

THE OBJECTIONS AND THE APPEAL

The first objections of Arjuna refusing to fight the foe are sudden and unexpected from a warrior aware of his part in the affairs of men. It is obvious that they are personal and domestic and sentimental but claim to have ethical and religious sanction by raising the cry of 'Dharma in danger.' In these utterances of Arjuna, depressed and despondent at the critical hour, Shri Krishna perceives clearly a confusion of issues, a self-delusion, a forgetfulness of the noble ideals of the hero remarkable for the type of heroism he represents. It ill becomes a warrior of Arjuna's birth, social standing, temperament and training, to shrink from the fight and refuse to have the honour and joy of doing his part in the task before him.

"This dejection is ignoble, un-Aryan," says the Lord, "surely this your resolve shuts against you the doors of Heaven that are open to the hero that does his part and obeys the law of his being. Indeed, this is infamous. Stand up; impotence does not befit you. How is it that you are weak-hearted at this hour of crisis?"

"How can I attack the venerated Bhishma and Drona?" cries Arjuna, "I prefer the beggar's bowl to blood-stained kingdom won by the slaughter of these Gurus, nor is it certain that mine will be the victory in the battle......It is true that faintness has overpowered me. I am confused as to which is Dharma, the law that I should obey; give me the decision. I am thy disciple, I have sought thee for guidance, give me thy word in the matter. But be pleased to know my attitude. My senses are dried up by this anguish; and I do not see if I can be cured at all either by an unrivalled monarchy on earth or by an overlordship of the gods in heaven."

Here it is necessary to note the three distinct but rapid steps in the development of Arjuna's psychology before the teacher finds him competent to receive the divine wisdom. It is in crises when one's strength is really put to test that one becomes aware of his weakness and defects of which he is normally unaware. Confident, self-reliant and valiant, Arjuna comes into the battle-field and becomes a prey to fears, doubts and despondency. Then having become conscious of his human limitations, ignorance, confusion and weakness, he makes a clean confession of them with courage, strength and total sincerity. Finally, he puts faith in the superior wisdom of his trusted friend and is prepared with an unquestioning obedience to submit to the decisive word of the divine guide to whom he offers to surrender his faltering will and indecisive judgment.

Shri Krishna listens to the words of Arjuna and is satisfied that his inner condition will enable him to receive the wisdom, the secret of action, the knowledge of the Law. When Arjuna first let drop his bow and refused to resist the enemy, he was self-assertive and unaware of his weakness and the Lord called upon him to get up and in words that sound like the command of an army officer ordering a soldier to go to the field and do his duty. Could it be really so? That was perhaps an apt reply, and Arjuna was rightly reminded of his own Dharma, the law of the Kshatriya when he enlarged upon the interests of Kuladharma and Varna-Dharma. Thus it was brought home to him how his Dharma as a Kshatriya conflicted with the Dharma of the Kula and the Varna, and he was awakened to a clash of Dharmas, the real basis of which he could not comprehend. "My notions of Dharma are confounding enough, *dharma-sammoodha-cetah,*" cries Arjuna, "teach me, I have sought thee for wisdom; *śiṣyaste ham śādhi mām tvām prapannam.*"

Hearing the words of Arjuna, the Lord smiles and says in effect: "You speak words of wisdom but are you really wise? The wise do not grieve either for the dead or for the living. You confess that you are weak and perplexed and ask me to give you my decisive word to guide you aright. You speak of Dharma without knowing what it really is. Now that you submit to my final decision, it is necessary that yours must be an intelligent submission to my word. There is great confusion in your mind about Dharma, which you yourself recognise. Your weakness is manifest in your sorrow and suffering for the living that are certain to die whether you will or will not do what in spite of you, you will be compelled to do by the Kshātra nature in you, the law of your own being, Swadharma. Each one has got to understand his own law of being and act in consonance with it. Surely I will help you to know the Dharma, the supreme law that is to govern all your action. I do appreciate the sincerity and earnestness of purpose with which you surrender your will and judgment to my guidance.

"But I do not want you to follow my lead blindly. You must have an intelligent appreciation of the whole position; you must know the various factors that have brought about the miserable confusion in your mind compelling you at the hour of action to an ignoble and unmanly resolve to withdraw from life's activity that is yours by the very nature and law and force of your being. And this infamous shrinking, you hope by mistake, would pass under the justifying guise of benevolence and compassion to your kindred, of dutiful reverence to elders and of religious regard for the sacred traditions preserved intact by society which would otherwise run to ruin. You also proclaim your ignorant and egoistic withdrawal as a big sacrifice in the cause of righteousness and are indeed perpared to forego the pleasures of royalty on earth and the coveted company and rulership of gods in heaven!"

At the close of the teaching when Shri Krishna has finished his say and answered the questions and cleared the doubts of Arjuna, the latter feels free to fight and tells the Teacher, "My delusion is dispelled; by your grace, Achyuta, I have recovered my sense." Now how did he begin to fight the battle? What was his attitude towards the terrible action he was to enter upon? What became of the ethical scruples and the sense of social danger that troubled him so much and served as a prop and excuse for his hesitation to fight and the resolve to retrace his steps?

His views of Dharma and Kàrma are now changed. He is now convinced that erroneous notions held him back from the free course of action dictated by the law of his being. The disillusionment came by the grace of the Divine guide in the light of the wisdom he received. The whole situation now presents a different view. There is a radical change in his outlook and understanding of men and things, of Dharma and Karma, of God, Nature and the meaning of life. He has now a knowledge of the principles of creation, of God, world and soul. And this supreme and authoritative knowledge of the Divine Lord Himself helps him in the part he is called upon to play, not for his personal gain, as he in his first delusion fancied, not for princely pleasures here or for heavenly happiness there. He knows the secret, the law of action and his own nature. His nature is sure to compel him into action whether he wills or not, and that nature of his is an instrument, an executive part of the supreme nature of the Lord. Action is inevitable in life. It is the true law of life to do works in the world in a divine spirit with a spiritual sense. He knows now that to get at the guiding principle of works he should no more think in terms of human relations and duties. Works he has to do according to his nature, but the fruit is to be left to the Lord of Nature that does the work. He is the willing and conscious instrument of the Lord to allow the nature in him to do the work, to fulfil the Law and purpose of the Lord through human life in the world.

In fact, life itself is a battle-field in which the sons of darkness, the Asuras, the ungodly forces of evil and wrong are arrayed against the sons of Light, the Devas, the spiritual and godly forces of the right and the good. Heroic Arjuna is to fight the battle of the Devas; his sense of good and evil, Dharma and Adharma grows with his developing knowledge of the true nature of the world, of himself and his Lord. He rejects the old notions of his egoistic reasoning from personal attachments and accepts the god-given knowledge of Dharma and Karma, of Yajna, Yoga and Sankhya. This gives him the wisdom that action done in devotion to the Divine helps the human soul to realise its consciousness in the divine glory of disinterested action and that the human soul in conscious union with the Lord of all works, does works, not for itself, but for the Divine Lord of the world as He too does work for the sustenance of the world. *Utsīdeyur ime lokāḥ na kuryām karma ced aham.*

THE QUESTIONS AROUND

**D.*—How is it that all on a sudden Arjuna became grief-stricken? He was a born hero; surely he must have considered the consequences before he shared the decision to fight that his brother Yudhishthira in council was forced to take.

M.—Arjuna was a blessed soul. Indeed his plight was a pity. It is always at a critical hour that the hidden forces of darkness and weakness manifest themselves. It was necessary that he should become conscious of them, and he had a rude awakening. But it was only the darkest hour before dawn. For, was he not immediately to receive the supreme wisdom of the Divine? What was lurking within had to come out. It was a blessing in disguise.

D.—Why should Arjuna be preferred to Yudhishthira by Shri Krishna for giving the teaching?

M.—He was best fitted for the divine work and wisdom. For Yudhishthira was too high above the average, already ruled by high ideals of saintliness and spiritual truth. Arjuna represents a higher type of the average and one aspiring to be ruled by lofty ideals with a large capacity to maintain the balance between the extremes.

D.—If this is all the reason, Shri Krishna could have instructed him on other occasions as they have always been friends.

---

*Discussion between the disciple (D) and the master (M).

M.—True. When we study carefully the character of Arjuna in the epic, we can say this is one plausible reason. This is not the only occasion when Shri Krishna gives his counsel to Arjuna. Here the kind of Yoga he teaches determines the choice of the occasion.

D.—It is admitted that they were friends. For that reason could he not have given previous assurance that he would be victorious over the enemy so that he might not have the doubt that he expresses whether he would win at all?

M.—Shri Krishna had given it and Arjuna knew it. At the exhortation of Shri Krishna, Arjuna, preparing to come to the battle-field, offered his worship to the Divine Mother Durga, and received Her blessings and boon of victory. Shri Krishna was present then and re-assured him. You find this notable incident in the closing part of the section preceding the Bhagavad Gita in the Bhishma Parva.

D.—Then how is it that Arjuna retraced his steps and found himself in a pitiable position?

M.—That is the wonder. It brings home to us in a striking manner the truth that even the man of high ideals is liable in moments of trial to be led away by undreamt egoistic tendencies from his avowed ideals that guide him in favourable circumstances. Man by his egoism asserts and re-asserts under many masks and is easily led astray, in spite of a god's guarantee, from the assured path of safety until he realises his vanity and ignorance and intelligently gives himself unreservedly to the guidance of a Higher Power as Arjuna gives himself to Shri Krishna.

THE AVATAR

D.—The Gita and the great epic in many places speak of Krishna and Arjuna as friends in a special sense. What is the character of this friendship?

M.—It represents a deeper truth than what appears on the surface. Of course it is an indissoluble bond of friendship. It is the relation of the aspiring soul and the compassionate Lord.

D.—Is that why they say Krishna and Arjuna are the inseparable Nara-Narayana?

M.—Yes. Nara is Arjuna. Narayana is Krishna.

D.—How could that be? Nara and Narayana seem to be the names of two Sages.

M.—That is true. The Mahabharata refers to them as having lived in a by-gone age; together they lived an austere life, in Tapas, in the Himalayas; and their names and the very spot had become so sacred that Yudhishthira during his Himalayan visit paid his homage to the holy hermitage.

D.—Then if it is a fact that Arjuna and Krishna were those two sages in a previous incarnation, what are we to understand when we are told that Shri Krishna is an incarnation of Vishnu and Arjuna is born of a part of Indra, *Indra-amśa*?

M.—Do you not find in the Gita that Shri Krishna himself says to Arjuna: "You and I have had many births; I know them, but you know not?"

D.—I want to be further enlightened on this subject of the births of God. It is profoundly interesting.

M.—This birth we call Avatar. It is a descent of God into the world to uplift it. Such an intervention from above is necessary at every crucial stage in the upward march of the world's progress. Now, evolution is a common concept in modern thought. How far the evolution theory of Natural Science is valid is a matter that need not concern us here. But there seems to be a secret, a philosophic truth, a spiritual sense behind it. The version of the Puranic legends of Avatar, however crude and allegorical in manner, is sufficiently suggestive of the ascending order of the graded development of the world-spirit. Do we not find something in this order of the Avatars beginning with the deluge—Matsya (the fish of the water), Kurma (the tortoise, both of land and water), Varaha (the boar, the beast of the land), Nrisimha, the lion-man, half human, Vamana the dwarf, the uncivil, violent and robust Parashurama, the well-disciplined, refined and royal Rama, and Shri Krishna, the yogin of high culture and spirituality?

D.—Granting that such a divine intervention from above forms part of the general scheme of things, how can we say that Shri Krishna refers to these incarnations, when he speaks of the many births of Arjuna and himself? Does it not mean the previous human births of both of them?

M.—Surely it does. It was simply to impress upon you the general truth about incarnation, pointing to the need of Divine advent into the world in crises that I referred to it. But here the Lord refers to human affairs and his many human births.

Speaking of his Yoga, he says: "I taught this Yoga to Vivasvān, Vivasvān gave it to Manu, and Manu to Ikshvāku and thus the wisdom was transmitted from age to age. When through the efflux of time the Dharma fades and Adharma prevails, I come down for the establishment of the Law, for the destruction of the wicked and the protection of the virtuous."

It is natural that Arjuna should be bewildered. How could Shri Krishna who was born yesterday have taught Vivasvān in an ante-deluvian age? Obviously Shri Krishna wants Arjuna to know that he was not confined to this single birth and had many births before.

D.—If Shri Krishna was the sage Narayana and Arjuna was Nara in previous birth, how could we speak of them together as Avatar Nara-Narayana?

M.—Both are divine in the sense that Nara is the Individual and Narayana, the Universal; the former is the mould of the human soul to work out and express the universality of the Divine, the latter is Parama Purusha, working out His will for His divine expression in and through the instrument and mould, the human soul, his own individual part, an eternal portion of Himself, *amśah sanātanah.* Thus the two, Nara and Narayana, are inseparable. The ideal type of the aspiring soul, a willing and conscious instrument is Nara, Arjuna, fostered and carried safe by the moving Spirit, the guiding Light, Shri Krishna, Narayana.

D.—Then is Nara-Narayana or Krishna-Arjuna only a symbol?

M.—It is a living symbol, an expression of a great spiritual truth. That does not necessarily mean that there is no historic basis for the story of the Avatar. The story could be of little value to us if the Avatar does not establish in our hearts and minds something of enduring value. Shri Krishna and Buddha and Christ are ideals enshrined in the human heart. Herein lies the meaning and purpose of incarnation, whatever might be the circumstances and details incidental to the outward activity and immediate effect of the life and influence of the Avatar.

D.—What then is the meaning of Krishna Avatar?

M.—The question is more easily asked than answered. People understand it according to their lights. That the destruction of Adharma and the establishment of Dharma is the purpose of true Avatar is a general dictum. It is not simply the destruction of a few thousands or lakhs of men on the Kaurava side representing Adharma that was the object of the Avatar, though that was a need and circumstance of the external conditions under which the message of the Avatar had to be given. Neither did the Kauravas monopolise all Adharma, nor has wickedness in the world been rooted out ever since. Positively, therefore, the character of the Dharma established is the subject of the Gita. This Dharma is understood in many ways and is discussed elsewhere. But one thing we may note here and that is that it is the Dharma of Nara-Narayana, the Krishna-Arjuna Yoga, the conscious union of the human soul with the divine Purusha in life and action. It is the Dharma or law of the human soul to allow itself to be guided by the Divine in life, not in its egoistic interests and for private profits, but for the sake of the Divine, as everything really belongs to Him.

D.—But why should they speak of Nara or Arjuna as an aspect or *kalā* of Indra, and of Shri Krishna as Parama Purusha, God Himself? What is the meaning of the many gods born into the world? After all, there is only one God.

M.—It is true that God is one and the sages call Him by many names. It is also true that He is named after His different aspects. But there is a still greater truth and this the modern mind is not yet fully ready to accept. God is the self of all the world and all that exists; and the gods are His various limbs and do their functions, *angāni anyāh devatāh.*

When I give you a blow with my hands, you may say my hand gives the blow and not any other limb.

All the same it is I that give the blow. The gods are distinct powers and personalities of the one God. When you and I can realise our inseparable unity in the divine Being, the gods who are much more powerful and knowing than we are, can they not in their own ways be in realised union with the one God and thus have the title to be worshipped as the Supreme God Himself? But, mind you, those gods do not depend for their existence upon our imagination. Of course there has been the tendency in us not merely to tolerate with philosophic indifference but positively to encourage the worship of god-forms as a concession to the limitations of the human mind and the yearning of the human heart. Any form can be used as a symbol for worship of the One and the Gita supports it. *Yo yo yam yam tanum bhaktah śraddhayārcitum icchati.* But this form-worship has nothing to do with the gods I speak of.

These gods are different from one another just as we are; only they are much more truly and flexibly nearer the one Supreme Being than we. You see the point?

D.—Then, is it polytheism?

M.—You may please yourself by calling it so; only it is not opposed to monotheism. In fact, you cannot label it as any 'ism'. The metaphysical mind of mediaeval India was satisfied with abstract ideas of the ultimate Truth, of the principles of creation, God, world and soul and constructed the philosophic systems of dualism and monism, qualified and unqualified. But the spiritual mind from the Vedic ages down to our own has not troubled itself about any 'ism.' It tries and gets the experience and puts it in the language of the age. It does not theorise or hunger for explanation. To it what matters is fact and experience rather than explanation and theory.

D.—What is the fact here about the gods?

M.—We have a number of hymns which we consider to be records of the religious experiences of the sages and these speak of the distinct character of the gods. As I have already illustrated from the *Taittirīya*, it is not difficult to reconcile these polytheistic conceptions with monotheistic or even monistic thoughts.

D.—Then what you say comes to this : that Arjuna who was the sage Nara in a previous birth is an Avatar of the Indra aspect of God.

M.—We need not attempt to fix now the exact sense of the aspect of Indra in the Veda. It is enough if we remember this much. As far as one can see, it is the Mahabharata that first speaks of the theory of *avatāra* and *amśa avatāra.*

D.—Do we elsewhere hear of these two sages Nara and Narayana, beyond the references in the Mahabharata?

M.—Rarely. But there is a sage Nara who is the seer of two hymns addressed to Indra. He belongs to the house of Bharadvaja. You find him in the sixth Mandala of the Rig Veda. Perhaps this seer Nara, devoted to Indra, was Arjuna in his next incarnation blessed and guided by the Indra spirit.

D.—This is interesting.

M.—You see if one is devoted whole-heartedly to an ideal, he is bound to realise it in the long run. Perhaps there was a certain contact of Indra established in Nara through his devotion and worship before he left the body and thus he was Arjuna in the next incarnation, chosen to express the Indra aspect of the Divine, guided by the Supreme Lord Himself.

D.—Can anything similar be said of the sage Narayana?

M.—Yes, he is the well-known seer of that wonderful hymn in the tenth Mandala of the Rig Veda, the Purusashukta.

D.—Why should you say wonderful? Every hymn is great in its own way.

M.—But this hymn reveals to us certain sublime truths which moulded the mind and soul of the nation for scores of centuries.

D.—What are they? Can you name a few?

M.—I shall just suggest briefly one or two points. It is this seer Narayana that gives us the great truth revealed to him, "The Purusha is all this, what has been and what is yet to be." Look at the grand idea. Don't you see how much it contains? Our modern thought of the Spirit in 'being and becoming' is only a philosophic concept with us. But with Rishi Narayana it was a substantial truth with body and soul, so to say. He was face to face with it. He saw and realised the truth and became one with the Purusha. Again, another grand idea of creation in this hymn is the sacrifice of the Purusha that makes creation possible. That is the ancient imagery. In our language we may say He gave himself to creation and became the world. Again the very body of the Purusha produces the four-fold human type. I have thrown out these suggestions; you can see how the Gita embodies these ideas in the language of the age.

D.—Can you give me references to the ideas stated above?

M.—Why, it is easy. Shri Krishna referring to *Cāturvarṇya*, the four Varnas, says, "They were created by me on the principle of the divisions of guṇa and karma, quality and works." As for the creation idea, you will see in the Gīta that the whole creation, Nature, is a small portion of Himself supported by His supreme power, *parā prakṛti*, *yogamāyā* and so on. Again, "I am *Uttama Puruṣa*," says Shri Krishna. This Purushottama idea, considered to be peculiar to the Gita, seems to have been first revealed to the world through Narayana, the seer. Of course in this Mantra of the Rig Veda you do not have the word *uttama*, but then the context there is, "all this is the one Purusha." Obviously God is the Uttama Purusha. When the Lord in the Gīta authoritatively asserts "I am the Purusha Uttama," we are reminded of the seer Narayana who realised his oneness with the supreme Purusha. To put it in other words, you may say God the supreme Purusha revealed or realised Himself in the human embodiment of the seer Narayana and since then Narayana has become the great name of Vishnu even as Vāsudeva has become the supreme name of God after the incarnation of Shri Krishna, son of Vasudeva.

D.—But the difficulty is, they give a different meaning to the name. Nārāyana is He whose abode is in the Nara, which term means, according to some, 'waters,' according to others, '*tattwas.*'

M.—That is the Puranic version. There is a symbolic sense in it. But Nara and Narayana are mentioned together as sages who lived as Tapasvins. But if we can rely upon etymological derivation of words, Nārāyana is the grandson of Nara. Perhaps they lived an austere life together; the former incorporated the supreme Purusha who appeared as Shri Krishna in the Mahabharata time; the latter worshipped and communed with Indra and by his grace and contact did his part in the field of life, Dharmakshetra, in the field of action, Kurukshetra. For, was it not the interest of Indra, the king of gods ever engaged in giving battle to Asuras, sons of darkness, to keep flying the flag of the sons of Light, of Dharma?

THE GITA AND THE COMMENTARIES

D.—Of the three orthodox schools of current philosophic thought, Dvaita, Vishishta-advaita and Advaita, which is the school that best represents the spirit of the Gita?

M.—The question raises a big controversy. Each school claims to give the right interpretation. The Gīta had become such an important scripture that a commentary on it was found indispensable for the Achāryas, especially as it contained certain apparently contradictory or irreconcilable statements, in certain places favourable, in others unfavourable to their schools. These Achāryas when they began to write their commentaries had their own rigid systems. It was their object to bring out a philosophic system of the Gita. But each had a school of thought to stand upon and naturally gave greater importance to the passages favourable to his position and treated others not so favourable as auxiliary and of secondary importance.

D.—Do you mean that none of the Bhashyas is faithful to the Gita?

M.—I do not mean that exactly. If some school is nearer the core of Gita's teachings than others, it is more because of certain aspects of the philosophic position of the school than because of the spirit in which these commentaries are written.

D.—How do you mean? Is the spirit of the Gita then not the same as that of the commentaries? Have we to reject the views of our great Achāryas? Could we be wiser than they?

M.—That the spirit of the Gīta is different from that of the commentaries is patent. Where do we find in these our philosophies that catholic, comprehensive and all-inclusive spirit of the Gīta? The Gīta is used as a battle-field in the commentaries where the authors engaged in controversial refutation of one another try to settle accounts. The Gīta intends to solve the problem of life from a divine and ideal view-point of man on earth. It gives a new meaning to the problem itself. It uses all the current metaphysical ideas, the many paths of knowledge, bhakti and other yogas, to expound the one yoga it has in view. It is the yoga or union of the human soul with the Divine spirit in life, the Divine driving the chariot and the human willing and acting for the purpose of the Divine. For this, faith and devotion to the Divine, *śraddhā* and *bhakti*, a dynamic and plastic yet firm and steady will to work, not in egoistic spirit but for God's purpose in the world, and a knowledge and growing consciousness of the Divine in the All and as the Supreme Self of the All are all necessary. Look at this yoga towards which all the teachings of the Gīta converge and compare it with the trenchant formulas of the philosophies and their tendency to drift more and more to hair-splitting.

We can use these views of the Achāryas according to our needs and light. Granting that we are unable to accept or follow their views to the end, we need not necessarily be wiser than they. Perhaps their dialectical warfare and intellectual subtleties with an imposing apparatus of technique in the realm of ideas were a response to the need of their age. We can hardly make any spiritual progress or even intellectual advancement if out of the natural and necessary reverence for the past we blindly believe that "all the great and good are dead and the living are totally depraved." The Gita discourages the idea that spiritual experiences and possibilities can be exhaustively stated even by the Veda, *jijnāsurapi yogasya śabda-brahma ativartate.*

Never perhaps in the known history of mankind were there greater opportunities for a wider intellectual awakening to the spiritual possibilities of man than to-day. Luckily, the days are gone, and are not likely to recur, when the aggressive type of ignorance in the extreme could hold out its hand and say, "All the truths are contained in my scripture. Whatever is not found in it must necessarily be untruth. Therefore it is wicked and presumptuous to differ from the written word of my text. Follow the trodden track. Thus far and no further."

D.—You don't attach importance to the commentaries?

M.—I do. The one point of value in them is that after all they accept the spiritual idea, though the trend of thought and the metaphysical bent may not contribute as much to the practical side as to the sharpening of the philosophic intellect. What I mean to say is this. Experience is synthetic; our mind is pre-eminently analytic.

In your zeal to climb the highest heights, you cannot afford to ignore the wider life around you, which too is God's creation and forms part of the Divine scheme. See the Gīta, see how it treats in a practical spirit, how it speaks of Samādhi, Yoga, and Jnāna, to be practised and realised here in life and not as something beyond, to be realised by shunning the world as an evil.

D.—After all it comes to this. Believe the Gita; it embodies the wisdom of Shri Krishna, God Incarnate.

M.—No. To the sceptic, we say, take the Gita for what it is worth, for the stuff it contains. It stands on a par, to say the least, with the highest wisdom in any of the world's great scriptures. But to the man of faith and understanding we would say, don't be carried away by wrong notions of the extreme sides. Surely it is the wisdom of the Avatar. The man of faith, the aspirant, the seeker after truth need not be disturbed by the views of the sceptic. Intellectual vanity is the most incorrigible of all human vanities. The sceptic boasting of his intellectualism may even accept God in theory and in the same breath, have his fling at "mysticism". The savage in the Sahara does not believe that water can freeze. Of course, he is honest. When he comes out of his desert home he can learn for himself that there are other climes where water really freezes. The dry-as-dust, self-sufficient intellect can but pose as the monarch of the metaphysical realm it surveys and can afford to deny in practice the recorded experiences of the past or present, if these do not fit in with its preconceived notions. But a robust and healthy intellect eager to be free from prejudices can always be of great help to spiritual growth, if it accepts in practice its limitations, and proceeds in earnest with openness to get at facts by experience and does not rest satisfied with dissection of facts into ideas of the mind.

D.—Did not then Arjuna fight the battle as part of the duty of the Kshatriya?

M.—Arjuna was born into the house of the fighting class, the Kshatriya. His temperament and qualities were best fitted to his birth in that age. The Kshatriya Dharma, the duty of the Kshatriya to society, he was forced to accept by an inner Dharma of the type of the human soul in him into which he had an awakening at the instance of his divine friend and teacher, Shri Krishna. There was no clash of the inner Dharma with the outer Dharma of the Kshatriya. Whenever such a clash arises, it is the inner law that should prevail to which preference is always given. This is the burden of the Gita's song. For it is through the awakening of his soul to the inner law of its being that man has to learn to do works in the world for the Divine and develop his consciousness towards union with the Divine in will, action and love. And nothing could be allowed to stand in the way of the inner law being fulfilled. Arjuna had to ignore the great moral law of non-killing, *ahimsā paramo dharmah.* He could not shrink from the *guru-hatyā*, the killing of the gurus, as the supreme Dharma must have its sway over all other human considerations. To check violence with violence was a necessary evil and the ancient social order devised a means by which a high purpose and moral tone and religious sense could govern the heroic type of man, free from ill-will and wileness or anything ignoble. Thus society was regulated and purged of weakness and violence alike, by a choice of the lesser evil of using a select section of the society to guard against the danger of the whole society falling a prey to wickedness and violence. However moralised and sanctified by ethics and religion, this organised homicide could hardly stand the test of a religious standard that professes to develop the finer and ethical sentiments of humanity.

But here, it was not an ethical expediency sanctioned by the practised religion of the social institutions of the day, rather it was a spiritual necessity for Arjuna to rise above the conventional and personal considerations of the conflicting duties and obey the inner law for a divine work. Therefore the sense of the Dharma used here is too broad to be narrowly confined within local and temporal limits. Surely the Gita would not find fault with a * Kaikeya Ashvapathi, a Kshatriya for not keeping his spiritual knowledge to himself but playing the role of the priest and the teacher, as that is not his *varṇa dharma.* It would not call upon a Shankara Acharya, the only son of his mother, to live a married life and perform † Agnishthoma and other rituals, if not to please the gods and go to heaven, at least for *citta-śuddhi*, and thus to contribute his quota to the ritualis-

---

* This is a reference to the Chandogya Upanishad.

† The non-performance of compulsory Vedic rites leads to *dharmabhramśa*, fall from Dharma, the religious path.

tic means of bringing down rains from the region of the gods. Many an instance in ancient history and in recent times can be seen of great men, devotees, men of wisdom and God-realisation and of vast spiritual influence, founders of religious sects, who became great, spiritual and godward and were benefactors of man and society, because they obeyed an inner law, a *svadharma*, an enlightened impulse from within and were guided by ideals befitting their nature, *svabhāva*. It is this Dharma of the inner man that the Gita places above the *grihya* or *smārta* or *śrauta dharma*, the household and social and Vedic duties of religious and social institutions. But these latter ought to be left undisturbed, as they are necessary for the mass, for the average man who is not awakened to a sense of this inner law to guide him in his life. He has to grow more and more unegoistic to learn the sublime law of work in the world. He has to subserve the interests of the family and of society, by doing works as his duty to them and to regard their rules and ideals as representing a part of the collective wisdom of the age until he is able to put forth something in return for what the society has done for him, by giving a further lead to its ideals and even changing the very face of it if need be. Freedom for individual growth and realisation of higher ideals ultimately benefit society even though the latter's rules and regulations for conducting its affairs may not always be conducive to the unstunted growth of the individual into the full stature of his being. Therefore the Gita while recognising the necessity for the imposition on the individual of the Dharma of society and its religion places above them the spiritual law of the soul's development which is a divine necessity in the upward march of man, the law which it calls its *svadharma*.

SANKHYA AND YOGA

We shall now proceed to the contents of the Gita.

In the *second chapter*, the Gita begins with the Sankhya Yoga in which it lays stress upon the Spirit imperishable in the perishing bodies. The Teacher calls upon Arjuna to keep to the unseen Spirit that endures in the seen forms of its embodiment. He addresses Arjuna upon the something in the body that persists and does not perish when everything else in it decays and disintegrates with it.

"Not that I never was, nor you, nor these princes; not that we all shall cease to be. Just as there is something in the body that possesses it and experiences the various stages of birth, growth and decay and survives them, so there is something that survives the perishing of the body too. The embodied soul grows in experience of bodily existence by a renewal of its forms through the device of death. Death is inevitable, for birth and death form the mechanism by which the bodily forms are renewed and manifested. Just as one throws off worn out garments to put on new ones, the soul changes its embodiment from the old to the new. The soul that is encased and involved in the body, trying to control and enjoy the bodily life, really supports itself from behind, from the something that is unmanifest, *avyakta*, from which all manifest beings come to be, and to which they return. The beginning and end of all manifest beings is that Unmanifest. It is all-pervasive and immutable. Keep yourself to it. You are that which does not perish. The sensuous touches cause heat and cold, pain and pleasure and all the pairs of opposites: They come and go; bear with them and realise that you are a soul-being with support in the Immutable. Do not be carried away by the appearance of birth and death. The Real in all that moves is your Self. To the unreal there is no existence; to the Real there is no cessation of existence. Know that the Spirit is neither killed, nor kills, nor causes to kill."

Then Shri Krishna ministers to the mentality of worldly wisdom by using persuasive words in the manner of the worldly wise and proceeds to say: "I have given thee this path of knowledge, the Sānkhya Yoga of the Jnānins. This path calls upon the soul to get extricated from the works of Prakriti, and cling to the spirit, Purusha, the eternal, unmanifest, unthinkable and unmodifiable."

The philosophy of Kapila is one of the six systems of ancient thought and is called Sānkhya, as it enumerates the Tattvas or cosmic principles that are 24 in number constituting what is called Prakriti, Nature. Purusha is the Spirit and is many. But the Sānkhya of the Gita is different; it uses the terms of the Sānkhya system and accepts its principle of the one Prakriti and many Purushas for practical purposes but proceeds further, as we shall see in the later chapters, notably the thirteenth.

Then the teacher proceeds to give the knowledge of Yoga. Literally yoga is union. It is not the yoga of

Patanjali which is the restraint of mind through concentration and trance, *samādhi.* Yoga is used in many senses. Each of the chapters of the Gita is named a yoga. For it is a great Yoga Shastra teaching the many methods of approach suited to the varying conditions and capacities of different temperaments and types aiming at the highest spiritual life, the union of the human soul with the divine spirit in will and knowledge. All the paths mentioned here—of knowledge, of devotion, of action, aim at union with the Divine. The Gita applies the term yoga to all the paths leading to God-realisation; but its reference to Karma Yoga as the yoga is necessitated by the path the Teacher has chosen for Arjuna, pre-eminently a man of action and devotion. This Yoga is to be practised in action by maintaining harmony and balance in the Reason, *buddhi,* that is nearer the Spirit whose will is poised in all the happenings in nature.

Before proceeding to expound the Yoga of action the Gita administers a rebuke to the Karmins, (*veda-vādarata*) the ritualists who hold that the performance of Vedic rites is the *summum bonum* of all Vedic wisdom. Their speech is flowery enough, but not fruitful. They are unwise, actuated by desire for happiness in other worlds; they insist upon the observance of ceremonials, but even these if done without desire can be turned to one's good. The ritualistic literature or rather the interpretation of these Karmavādins justifies the inferior place allotted to the Vedas, as their ideals, according to themselves, are enjoyment subject to Nature, Prakriti of the three gunas. Arjuna is called upon to rise above this lower Prakriti and to turn his back upon these Vedas which according to these learned interpretations give indulgence to the play of the inferior nature. It is necessary here to remember that the Gīta enters this protest only to redeem the true spirit of the Veda; for it is with great reverence for the Vedic wisdom that it refers to the Rishi, the Deva and the Chandas.

The Buddhi or wisdom that was given in dealing with the Sānkhya Yoga or the path of knowledge is not opposed to or really different form the wisdom that is now to be given for application in the practice of the path of Yoga. Shri Krishna calls it Buddhi Yoga here, for it is the *buddhi*, the pure reason, which implies a will in the intelligence that makes Karma Yoga possible. The knowledge given in the path of the Sānkhyas is to be applied in the path of Yoga which consists in the intelligent will lifted up and purified by a clear understanding of the Purusha, the Spirit, unmoved and unaffected by the play of Prakriti, Nature. What is necessary then, is a calm and firm will in the intelligence to maintain the balance amidst the changing modes of the play of Parkriti (of the three gunas *). Yoga brings a harmony between the theory and practice of knowledge. The two paths are different in method indeed, but they lead to the same goal; even on the way, one is implied in the other; even the Jnānin who is settled

* Rajas, Tamas and Sattva are the three qualities of Prakriti. They are the active, inert and comparatively calm and luminous modes of the play of Nature both in the inner and the outer existence.

in spirit and whose temperament and nature incline him less and less towards outward activity does the minimum of work needed for the sustenance of bodily life but is not affected by this work of Nature in him. Whatever work he does, he knows that it is not he that does the work, but it is Nature in him that does it and he is conscious of himself as firmly settled in the Self. The path of the Karmayogin begins with an intelligent will to maintain the balance between the pairs of opposites and thus to learn to do work without attachment to its fruit. By a habituated unattachment to the result of works the yogin raises his will with a purified understanding to a level from which he does his works. He is well poised in the spirit to maintain harmony between what he knows and what is done, between pain and pleasure, success and failure, gain and loss. To be thus poised in the Spirit and to do works is to gain skill in works. This skill gives a clear and practical knowledge of the spirit's equality in the opposites of heat and cold, grief and joy, or success and failure. Therefore yoga is described to be "skill in works", *yogah karmasu kauśalam.* Yoga is called equality, *samathvam yoga ucyate.* The teacher calls upon Arjuna to do works in the spirit and understanding of the principle of equality that gives a harmonising and balancing skill in action. Action thus done ceases to be a bondage for the doer of works.

Therefore karma, the Teacher says, is far inferior of Buddhi Yoga, the yoga of the intelligent will. Once you get the Buddhi, the pure reason, you know how to do works unattached to their fruits. The Gita gives a description of the character and condition of the sage to show how the Buddhi spoken of here is as indispensable for the Jnānin as for the yogin and that Samādhi is a state common to both, for it is in Samādhi as described in the Gīta and not in that of our popular misconceptions of it, that the Buddhi becomes free, firm and steady and the yogin is settled in the Brahmic state and Brahmic consciousness in whatever outward condition he may be.

"The Muni, the sage, is he who abandons all desires, and finds joy in the self by the self; for his understanding is well poised in the self. The sage is he whose mind is free from sorrow amidst miseries; equally free from desire amidst pleasures; he has no attraction, fear, or anger: firm and unshakable is his understanding. Everywhere unattached, he takes good and evil as they come, neither welcomes the one nor repels the other. Like the limbs of the tortoise his senses are drawn in from their objects on all sides; well poised is his understanding. . . . Sensual objects can be rejected by effort, but the relish or craving for them ceases only when one sees the Supreme. . . . One should know by a close reasoning the true cause of the roving habit of the mind. The mind is forcibly dragged by the senses in spite of one's efforts. To check them one has to be in yoga (yukta) with me, the goal," says the Lord. "When once the senses are under control, one is stable in mind. Reflection on sensual objects results in attachment to them; attachment gives rise to desire, desire brings forth anger, anger produces delusion, delusion causes confusion in memory which in its turn leads to the ruin of reason, Buddhi, and when Buddhi perishes one goes to perdition. Therefore, one must regulate * the sense-activities by clearing the senses of the impurities of attraction and repulsion and making them a kind of impersonal functioning. Thus the mind of man becomes supremely limpid and calm, while his senses are thus purified and allowed to graze upon their objects under the control of the self.

"In that calm, miseries vanish and in the calm and clear mind, the Buddhi reigns supreme. But Buddhi is impossible for the *ayukta*, for the unbalanced . . . He that has self-conquest is awake in That which is night to other beings; and where these beings are awake that is night to him.†

"Like the ocean which is full and not moved by the rivers flowing into it, the Jnānin is he into whom desires flow without affecting him. Such a one gets the Peace and not he that desireth desires. Abandoning all desires he moves about and yearns for nothing. He has no 'Mine' and 'I'. Unegoistic, he is firmly settled in the Peace."

Thus the chapter closes with the description of the Brahmic state which essentially lies in the supreme

---

*The Gita prefers this method to that of suppression of sense-activities: *Kevalairindriyaiścaran*.

†The Jnanin is aware in the Brahman: therefore he is awake in it. Others are unaware of it; therefore, they are in the dark. These are aware in the Ignorance in which the Jnanin does not live.

peace in which the understanding of the sage is well poised, whether he is active or otherwise, or in whatever activity he is engaged.

*KARMA AND YAJNA**

Shri Krishna has spoken so high of the path of Knowledge, of Jnāna and Samādhi, the natural and settled state of the sage, the supreme peace in which he acts and moves and lives undisturbed by material or mental movements amidst which he maintains a supreme poise in the all-pervading spirit, that Arjuna is naturally tempted to prefer this to the ghastly action to which Shri Krishna induces him. Here are two paths, Karma Yoga for the yogins, Jnāna Yoga for the Sānkhyas, says Shri Krishna. Don't imagine that abstaining from activity gives Naishkarmya, freedom from the bondage of action; nor does one realise the goal, Siddhi, by outward renunciation. No one can remain without action even for a moment. It is the compelling force of the qualities of Prakriti that causes the doing of works and every one is helpless and submits to this. Even if one suppresses his physical activity as a means of Jnāna and closes his eyes, with his mind still dwelling on the objects of sense, he is under a great delusion if he thinks that he is free from activity. Activity is not merely physical and outward, gross and visible motion; it is also mental and subtle, felt and unobserved. The ways of Prakriti are too subtle for observation by the mind given to the senses. It is only an intelligent will in the reason, Buddhi, that is above the senses and mind and is close to the

*Third Chapter.

Spirit, the Purusha, that can observe the workings of Prakriti. Therefore Buddhi Yoga is necessary. To do works united to the Buddhi, elevated above the mind, is indispensable and this Buddhi is as much necessary to the path of knowledge as to that of yoga. Only in the former there is an indifference to action, while in the latter there is a will enlightened and heightened, ready for the application of the spirit of knowledge in life, in works. In practice, therefore, it is first the mind that must refuse to give itself to the sense-channels that are subjected to the vital impurities of craving and aversion, attraction and repulsion; first this impurity in the channels of the senses must be removed by the refusal of the mental support to them and they must be trained for a free, pure and well-regulated functioning, not guided by motives and passions, but as a course of Nature's function in the body responding to the external Prakriti.

As it is impossible for anyone to be really inactive, as Prakriti is all the while busy with her own play even in the man who has either no capacity to know her subtler ways or has withdrawn his will to observe them, the best way to do works in the world is to consent to Prakriti's play without a desire for enjoyment of the fruits of works, leaving them to the Divine Lord of Nature. Why should the fruit of action be left to the Divine? It is the law of life that works must be done as a sacrifice and it has two aspects. Negatively, I lose what I give away; positively, it goes to him to whom it is given. To whom then should this sacrifice be offered? Obviously to the Divine Lord of the worlds and the gods and of all works, as He is the Lord of Sacrifice and of works; for it is really His Prakriti that does the works.

In the second chapter, at the commencement of the exposition of the Buddhi Yoga, which is the soul of Karma Yoga, the Gita flings a reproach at the presumptuous creed of the ritualist who has appropriated the word 'karma' and uses it to mean Vedic ritual, Vedic karma alone. Here it enlarges upon Yajna and uses it in an extended sense as it does the word karma. Whatever was the significance or symbolic sense of the Vedic Sacrifice in the mind of the ancient mystics and seers of the Mantra, as is really suggested in the Āranyaka literature, in the popular mind the sacrifice was a Vedic ritual to be performed by the higher classes to please the gods who in their turn shower their blessings upon earth. This popular notion is indeed supported by the learned interpretation of the Karmavādins. This is the most favourable presentation of the creed of ritualism, though even this position is not always free from the principle of legalising personal motives and desires for celestial enjoyments actuating the performance of sacrificial rites. This idea the Gīta dismisses and condemns in an unqualified manner, as it encourages the vitalistic and egoistic tendencies of man binding him to the wheel of lower nature and the gunas, freedom from which is essential for the redemption and uplift of the human soul that consents to be so low and unspiritual. And the Gīta re-discovers for us the essential sense of the ancient sacrifice, renews and extends it, and the Yajna that it teaches is for observance not by the select few, but by all the peoples. It gives a skilled touch to the ancient works and transforms their spirit for universal application and approval. God created 'the peoples and the sacrifice together,' it says; men have to give themselves to the gods and the gods increase thereby; the gods in their turn give themselves to men and the men increase. Thus the sacrifice becomes the 'cow of plenty'. This sense of sacrifice suggests a law of interchange between gods and men.

The ancient conception of the cosmos had it that there are distinct God-powers and God-personalities ruling the worlds and that all the worlds with all their beings and energies really belong to them and are ruled by them at the Will of the One God of all existence and of all the gods, who are but His nearer and diviner and self-conscious entities, powers and parts of Himself. Therefore man given to the doing of works compelled by inevitable nature, has to realise that nothing really belongs to him; his very body composed of the elements, the life-force in it, and his mind form but a part and product of the universal energy which is but a mode of Prakriti in the language of the Gīta, and the workings and belongings of gods in the ancient conception. Thus we find the justification of works done as sacrifice to the gods. We give to the gods what is their due and they are pleased, delighted and increase towards us, coming down to approach us for our offering. Nor are we utter losers for the giving. We lose what is selfish and lowly, human and dark and defective in us, only to gain our place with the gods, to grow more and more towards them; thus we too increase, proceed upwards. This is the law of 'give and take' between men and gods, this is the sense, spirit and justification of sacrifice that is so wonderfully expounded in the Gita and it adds that this spirit of sacrifice must move every work done by man, it is the law, and whoever does not fulfil it and arrogates to himself the fruit of his works fancying the world to be a field created for his personal profit and does not give the gods what is their due is verily a thief.* Whoever does not follow† this wheel of the Divine, the wisdom born of Him that is all-pervasive, and the law of sacrifice supported by that wisdom, whoever is given to sensual pleasures in a life of sin without regard to this,—really there is no meaning in his living. *Aghāyur indriyārāmo mogham pārtha sa jīvati.*

Just as the conception of the sacrifice as a rite is supplanted by this fresh spirit, that of the *nityakarma* of the Veda gives place to the *niyatakarma* of the Gita. *Niyatakarma* is regulated action. Elsewhere we have it that it is the action regulated by one's inner nature and law and way of being. The terms, *sahajam karma*, *svabhāva-niyatam karma*, *prakṛteh gunaih kriyamāṇanī karmāṇi*, prove beyond a shadow of doubt what the Gita means by *kāryam karma*. One has to regulate his action by a high sense of duty, by a constant reference to the Shastra and educate his will and conquer his ego to subserve a higher Will in his own supreme interest. But this is not the last word. For in course of

---

**Yo bhunkte stena eva sah.*

†*Akṣara-samudbhavam Brahma, Brahma-samudbhavam karma.*

time he grows to a sense of what it is tnat does the work and is active, and finds for himself the true law of his own inner nature and being. Until this is done it is a necessity that he should abide by the best traditions and ideals of the society, by the Shastra. The ordinary man, even he that is attached to works and their fruits must be allowed to have his way. He has to grope in the dark and grow. For how else is he to shake off his tamas, inertia? Even works done with attachment to fruits do good to him. Such a one shall not be disturbed in his ignorance. The wise man can even encourage him by himself doing works, but in his own way, free from attachment. The great man of ideals influences others by precept and example. His word becomes the law for others. Shri Krishna does not cease to do works. If he ceased to do them, the worlds would perish at once. For others he does work. The devotee with faith in him has to do works even as his Lord does. He too can have no attachment to the fruit. But he has a divine interest in the work. As the Lord Himself does not withdraw from work in the world and also because action is indispensable for life on earth, he has to grow in consciousness to share the work of the Divine Lord of works. That is the ideal of Karma Yoga that Shri Krishna came to establish or re-introduce into the world. Whatever may be the ideal of the spiritual man, to retire from life or cease to be active and shrink from the Divine works, from egoistic motives and interests, under the great delusion that knowledge consists in the withdrawal from action, can never form part of the spiritual ideal for the heroic type of man like Arjuna.

Then the fact is stressed that even the Jnānin who retires from life and has no human interest in it does work and is really active in his own way according to the nature in him. . . .

Of the three gunas of Prakriti, it is Rajas, the active principle that works under the garb of anger and desire and throws a veil of ignorance over the light of the Purusha; it is like smoke over the smouldering fire. Therefore the Spirit must be seen, the Purusha who is above the Buddhi, the mind and the senses; only when He is perceived, can one freely and easily settle oneself in the Buddhi and use the enlightened will to keep the mind calm and control and purify the senses.

THE FOURTH CHAPTER

The yoga of works as a sacrifice, says Shri Krishna, is an ancient one: He, the Lord, gave this yoga in the beginning to Vivasvan, he gave it to Manu, and Manu to Ikshvaku and thus it was handed down from age to age. When through ages its spirit is weakened and forgotten, the Lord has come again to give it to Arjuna. Arjuna now learns why the Lord takes on births: He is born again and again, when Dharma fades and Adharma prevails, for the destruction of the wicked and protection of the virtuous, for the establishing of the Law, the Dharma. We have already dealt with the subject of Avatar and the character of the Dharma he came to deliver. The Avatar is a mystery and so is his work. How can God, the ever unborn and endless take on births? It is the mystery of mysteries. The appearance of the world, the creation, this cosmos itself is a great miracle; and the manifestation in it of life and mind and man is a greater wonder still. The Infinite Divine, limiting Himself to finite form for a definite end again and again, is the greatest of all mysteries which it is impossible to unravel even for the wisest among men. "Whoever knows my Divine birth and Divine work," says Shri Krishna, "ceases to come again to birth: he comes to me. Free from anger and fear and passion, they, the many pure souls of Jnāna and Tapas, filled with me, have become part and parcel of myself." . . . It is not necessary that every man should be a *jnānin* or *tapasvin*. "In whatever manner men approach me, in the same manner I welcome them. It is my path everywhere that they follow."

Then the disputed question of God-created Chaturvarna (the four castes) is summarily explained as representing four types of men according to the character of the quality and activity that they predominantly put forth. The phrase *guṇakarma vibhāga* gives a universal aspect to the question of *varṇa* applicable to men in general as manifesting a divine principle in creation in many types, roughly classified as four, in which certain kinds of quality and activity preponderate over the others. It is interesting to note here, that Acharya Sāyana, the author of the great Vedic commentaries that have proved to be the stronghold of conservative forces and ritualistic creeds, comments upon the word Purusha in the Purusha Sukta, that He is the collective or universal being, Virat, *sarvaprāṇi samaṣṭhirūpah puruṣo virāt ākhyāyate*. But just as the Gita redeemed Yajna, Karma and Dharma from the narrow and limited groove of local and institutional rites, so it delivers Varna from the conventional sense obtaining in a limited geographical expression, into a vast and world-wide sense applicable to mankind.

Then we are given a large view of the Jnāna of the Karma yogin as well as of the Karma of the Jnāna yogin. Shri Krishna himself does works and has nothing to gain from them. Arjuna is called upon to know that the ancient sages from time immemorial have done works and were not bound by them. Therefore Arjuna, says the Lord, must do works likewise. Even the great seers know not what *karma* (action) is and *akarma* (inaction) is. One must know of right action and wrong action (*vikarma*, a rare phrasing) and inaction. Really, the course of Karma is impenetrable. * The wise man is he who sees action in inaction and sees inaction in action; he is *yukta* (united to me or balanced in me) and so is the doer of all works.

Before it closes, the chapter makes a free use of the figure of sacrificial offering in making mention of the various disciplines and activities including the regulation of Prāna and thus establishes the supremacy of sacrifice is its own sense of the term. It concludes that renunciation of works, if done at all, should be done by yoga alone where wisdom reigns and dispels doubts: nor is action a bondage. . . . The man that has faith and sense-control gets the knowledge leading to the supreme Peace. But the ignorant man, without faith and full of doubts goes to destruction, he has neither this world nor the next. Therefore cut off, says the Lord, with the sword of knowledge the doubt lingering in the heart, born of ignorance, and settle yourself in yoga. Stand up.

*The yogin sees the silent Self, the Purusha, in Nature, Prakriti that is active: there he is said to see inaction in action. He also sees the ever active Prakriti in the immutable Spirit that is the support of her activity, so he is said to see action in inaction.

*KARMA AND SANYASA**

The Gita avowedly preaches the gospel of action, but is not bigoted, and does not call upon every man of spiritual ideal to take to Karma Yoga, without regard to his aptitude, temperament, capacity, tendency, and the conditions incidental to human life in its particular environment, though it surely urges upon us to recognise the law, the incessant movement of Nature in the inner and in the outer, in the material body, mind and life and says that none, not even the Jnānin can escape the minimum activity indispensable for bodily life. It has a high place for the Jnānin and for the path of knowledge, even when it turns its back upon life and work. *Karmasanyāsa* (renunciation of works) and *karmayoga*, both are good and lead to the same goal. They are children who prate that Sānkhya and Yoga are different. But *karmayoga* is preferable to *karmasanyāsa*, says the Lord. For real Sanyasa is not an external affair; it is an inner condition. Know him to be in the unceasing Sanyasa who is untouched by desire or hatred. Sanyasa is not easy, one cannot get it without yoga. It is yoga that gives self-mastery, sense-control and self-purity. The yogin is untouched by the work he does. His Self is the Self of all beings. He knows the essential truth in all. He does not do anything; yet he sees, hears, touches, tastes and smells, eats, drinks, moves, breathes and sleeps. He speaks, gives and takes, closes and

*Fifth Chapter.

opens his eyes; he knows and holds the truth that the senses move to their objects.

. . . The eyes of the sage are filled with the spirit of equality, which is not merely an idea in his mind. He is firmly settled in the one Brahman that is equal in the many; and one with Brahman, he looks with an equal eye upon all, the learned Brahman and the lowly outcaste, the dog and the cow and the elephant. . . They have conquered everything in creation, here on earth, who are settled and well balanced in Brahman.

The way of equality is suggested here as a discipline in yoga and it is stressed in the sixth chapter as an important element in sādhana. The chapter closes with a statement of the character of the sage whose reason, mind and senses are regulated and under control and from whom are removed fear and hatred and anger. Therefore such a sage is *sadā mukta*, ever liberated. He gets the Peace knowing that the Divine is the enjoyer of all sacrifices and austerities and the great Lord of all the worlds and the friend of all beings.

*YOGIC DISCIPLINE**

The inward character of yoga and *sanyāsa* has been so clearly expounded that the Gita now emphatically affirms its conclusions that Sānkhya and Yoga are really one and that renunciation is not external in character nor does it come by the abandoning of religious rites or prescribed duties. No yoga is possible without inner renunciation which alone brings the quiet within. Action done renouncing the result becomes a means for the sage that aspires for yoga; the inner quiet that yoga gives is the means for the sage who has ascended the heights of yoga. He is said to have climbed up to yoga who has given up the running habit of the mind and its constructions and who is not bound by works or the objects of the sense-field. One must help oneself and get above depression. . . . The Self is the friend as well as the enemy. It depends upon one's alertness, ideals and aspirations. If the ego, the lower self, is subdued and brought under control, the higher Self is there ever in Peace, unruffled by the dualities of pain and pleasure and the like reigning in the lower life. The most effective discipline for yoga is to allow one's self to be guided by a spirit of equality, since Brahman is equal in all inequalities. God is immanent in every being and form and all beings are equally in Him. Therefore to look upon all as residing in the One and on the One

*Sixth Chapter.

Divine as residing in all beings, fills the mind with the idea of the supreme One amidst all differences. But how to do this is the question. To have an intellectual conviction is not enough; it can easily remain as an idea without any corresponding change in the outlook in practical life. The Gīta here makes a brief reference to certain religious yogic disciplines, notably Patanjali's system of psychological control, but uses them in its magnificent spirit of sifting the principles underlying the system of rules and methods of the *aṣṭānga yoga* and applying them for a higher yoga of *samatā*, equality.

A pure and quiet atmosphere is necessary for the practice of the yoga sādhana by which the mind is controlled. And the yogin must regulate his life by the golden mean of moderation in diet, in sleep and in all the necessary movements of life. His seat must be neither too high nor too low, neither too uncomfortable nor too comfortable. He shall not swing to the extremes of mortifying fasts and sumptuous feasts. He must be calm and cheerful and have in a fair measure all requisites for a life of mental and moral elevation without fear or desire disturbing his quiet. His mind must be one-pointed (preferably the thought of the Divine must fill his mind; *mat-citta*, says Shri Krishna). When the unsteady mind moves about, the yogin must be watchful and carefully draw it in from where it goes to the point it left. Every time the mind is moved by its own constructions or tossed by desires the yogin with a firm will grasping the intelligence, Buddhi, must slowly and quietly bring it back to the state of tranquillity. When the mind becomes as steady as the lamp in a windless place, it is said to be perfectly under control and it does not throw out waves. The yogin then begins to experience a supersensual delight. He finds this a great gain and a greater gain, he feels, there cannot be. Therefore, positively, a supreme delight possesses the yogin, while negatively he is rid of all desires and passions and attachments and impurities. Thus one is best fitted to be in Yoga, united to the Self, for the intense joy of the Infinite, the Eternal Brahman.

The fruit of such disciplines the Gita applies to the building up of the Sāmya yoga, the yoga of *samatā* or equality, which it considers to be not merely an effective means but a necessary basis for a spiritual life of knowledge and action, (Jnana yoga and Karma yoga) culminating in a real Bhakti, in a supreme love and devotion to the Divine, which, it often repeats, the Jnanin alone can have in a full measure. For, the *prapatti*, absolute and unreserved surrender to the Divine is possible for the Jnanin alone who has realised that all is Divine and in the Divine. Hitherto the Gita spoke of Jnana and Yoga as two different paths aiming at an inner quietism, at once a means and basis for action. Now from the seventh to the twelfth chapter the teacher gives the spirit, sense and justification of the Bhakti Yoga. Therefore the Lord urges that the sadhana of *samatā*, equality, is great and effective. "See the Self that abides in all beings. See that all beings abide in the Self." Thus the yogin sees the same everywhere. "Whoever sees Me everywhere and sees all things in Me, is never lost to My sight, nor am I lost to his vision. For I am ever in Him and He is ever in Me."

Arjuna asks: "If one has faith but has no strength for self-control and is unable to practise this *samatā*, the *sāmya yoga*, what is his fate, my Lord?" And we have the re-assuring word of Shri Krishna, "How can he of faith perish either in this life or in the next? Such a one comes back and is born into favourable surroundings or into the very house of yogins and then he is guided by the force of the past without any effort. Even he that wishes to know yoga gets beyond the Vedas. . . . . . All the yogins are great indeed, but he is greater than the rest who adores me with his inner self, given to me in great faith and devotion and he in my view is the most perfectly united to me."

*THE HIGHER AND THE LOWER NATURE**

Faith in the Lord and devotion to Him have been briefly mentioned and suggested as necessary but only the seventh chapter begins to harmonise knowledge with devotion and to broadbase Bhakti on the sure foundations of knowledge.

What we call the world, sentient and insentient, is made up of eight principles, constituting what is called the lower nature, *aparā prakṛti:* earth, water, fire, air, ether (*ākāśa*), reason (*buddhi*), mind, and ego (*ahamkāra*)—these are the eight that combine in varying proportions to bring into being numberless forms and countless species by the play of the three gunas or qualities. All existences are subject to the rule of the three gunas which are but the changing modes of this Prakriti that is universal. Sattva, Rajas and Tamas are present in and dominate all existence, one prevailing over the others. In external nature, Tamas, the principle of inaction or inertia, is dominant in the rock and the mineral; Rajas is predominant in the vegetable and the lower animal; Sattva in the higher animal, man. Again if we look at man in his natural being, with a body and life and mind, mind represents the luminous principle of Sattva; life, that of activity Rajas; and body, the principle of darkness and inertia, Tamas that is averse to change. Thus all nature is governed by the mecha-

*Seventh Chapter.

nism of this three-fold Prakriti, called the lower nature. But this natural machine is not self-sufficient. It is endowed with the capacity to subject all beings to its rule. Every being involved in it obeys it and is driven along its ways; even the mind and the Buddhi form part of this mechanism of Nature. Therefore it is stated elsewhere "Beings follow Nature. What can restraint do?" *Nigrahah kim kariṣyati?*

But is there no escape from this determinism of Nature? There is, if you choose. This lower Prakriti is guided by a different and higher Prakriti of the Divine Lord from above. He is not involved in it. It is his higher nature, Parā Prakriti, that upholds the whole world of the lower nature, Aparā Prakriti, and has really become the jiva, the life principle forming and sustaining it, *jīvabhūtā*. Therefore it is this *daivī prakṛti* of the Lord that works through the three gunas in the lower nature to educate the will and reason and ego involved in it by giving a sense of freedom to work and choose between right and wrong, good and evil, by the spell of the Divine illusion, Maya, *(guṇamayī prakṛti)* flung far and wide over the whole nature. Therefore the three gunas forming the mechanism of the lower Prakriti are really derived from the Divine Maya, *daivī, guṇamayī, mama māyā*, for delivering the being out of the darkness of the lower into the light of the higher part of the Supreme Divine.

It is to teach and establish, by precept and influence, by example and living guidance, the uplifting law, the Dharma that brings deliverance to the struggling soul in nature, that the Lord takes on human births from time to time and yet man in his egoism and ignorance denies him. "The wicked and the foolish with āsuric nature do not submit to me for deliverance," says the Lord, "for their knowledge is taken away by māyā."

"..... The fools do not recognise me because I am garbed in human birth, *mānuṣīm tanum āśritam.* They do not understand my supreme being, *param bhāvam*". But the good, the great, the wise, and the blessed always adore him. Roughly, there are four classes of devotees; those who worship him for relief from sorrows and sufferings; those that adore him to gain some worldly end in life; those that seek to know Him; and those that have realised Him. All are great and noble indeed. Even the man that approaches God in good faith, though he worships him with earthly motives, is infinitely superior to the man who is a beggar at the doors of the rich and the influential and cringes for worldly favours from a worldly being. God is the friend of all beings and of his devotees in particular, whatever may be their drawbacks, whatever may be the motive that induces them to approach Him. He knows best to deal with them, to deny or grant their prayers and take them into Himself, once they have the needed faith, strength, and devotion to approach Him with or without motive. The very fact that the God-idea dawns on the needy soul, whatever the need may be in its first approaches, is enough to take it Godward. Therefore the Lord says, all these devotees are noble, *udārāh sarve,* but the Jnanin is the greatest of all. "He is myself. He has realised all as the Divine, *Vāsudevah sarvam iti.* He knows nothing but the Divine. He sees everything as Divine and in the Divine. He is the greatest Bhakta." . . . But all devotees cannot be Jnanins. Therefore in whatever form or aspect the devotee approaches the Lord and offers his worship, He accepts it and takes the soul unto Him.

*THE IMMUTABLE BRAHMAN**

The Jnana yoga of the Gīta, grasped in a large and free spirit, leads to the highest form of Bhakti, even as Bhakti in its highest term *prapatti* gives the fruit of the path of knowledge. The seventh chapter spoke of the Lord of Prakriti, higher and lower, of the power of the Lord of deliverance in the higher Nature and of the power for bondage locked in the lower Nature, guided, indeed covertly, by the divine Maya. The guiding spirit, the life-principle of the lower Nature, has been stated to be in the higher divine Prakriti that is not involved in the world but is always free and above. But even in the world, in this Prakriti which is openly or secretly mobile, *kṣara*, there is something which is the support of all this mutable existence. This something is in the lower Prakriti here, in the higher Prakriti there; it is everywhere but is not particularly related to any manifestation of Prakriti. It is all-pervasive, free, eternal, unmanifest being, *avyakta*. This is called the *akṣara*, immobile in all that is mobile. It is unmanifest amidst manifestations, unperishing amidst all that perish, indifferently supporting all, itself without support. It is equal in all, *samam Brahma*. It is called the unmanifest and immutable Self, *avyakta*, *akṣara*. The Gīta recognises this great Truth, the realisation of the sages and says: "This is the supreme station, *Param Dhāma* of

*Eighth Chapter.

the Divine. For whoever reaches this immutable state has no necessity for re-births." This statement about the *akṣara parabrahman* or the immutable Supreme is necessary in view of what the Gita has stated in the previous chapters and of what it has got to say later. For the Lord says this is a difficult path and the better way that he expounds later is preferable to this. But it recognises the importance of this exalted state and the profound truth of this intensest and deepest realisation of the Self in the Impenetrable, the Unmanifest.

o o o o

The Gita in the *ninth chapter* develops the theme of the path of Bhakti by giving an account of the all-powerful character of the Divine Lord of all the worlds, and his eternal and absolute freedom from all creation and of his readiness to descend to the level of the human consciousness and take the human birth to uplift the lower world. It concludes with a great verse which we find repeated in the closing words of Shri Krishna in the eighteenth chapter: "Become my-minded, be devoted to me performing works as sacrifice and submit yourself. Thus with your self united to Me, you reach Me, having Me for the supreme goal."

*THE VIBHUTI**

We have seen how the way of equality was preached as a great sadhana, the discipline of looking upon the Self in everything and everything in the Self. But this way suits the capacity and temperament of the Jnana yogin and for the devotee is enjoined a constant meditation on the Divine. How is such a sadhana possible with our eyes wide open to a world of stern realities staring us on all sides, presenting a variety of things and beings and forms in different kinds and qualities that excite in us dissimilar sensations, feelings and sentiments? Now it is sweet and pleasant and lovely, or powerful and terrible and vehement, now it evokes sympathy and pity, again it is wonder and curiosity, or it is funny and humorous and attractive, again it is disgusting and contemptible. Such is the world: it presents a terrible, undivine and unspiritual front at every turn, and how can we see the Divine in these cruel realities of the world of God's creation? The theory of *vibhūti* offers a solution to the devotee to seize upon the Divine in everything that faces him in the world, through the central and typical manifestations, called the Vibhutis. He is to look upon the world, not as a general manifestation of the Divine,—for, the whole world is that—not in the disorderly and chaotic form it presents to a confused mind in its crude workings through its senses,

*Tenth Chapter,

but in the concentrated expression of a divine quality of strength breathing out a divine light and glory, in its cosmic aspect compelling the open heart of the devotee, of the God-lover, to draw from it the peace, power and joy of the Divine. The Vibhuti is the manifest stress of the power and light, of many a divine quality bespeaking the glory of the Divine residing and revealed in the essential, powerful, lovely and luminous aspects of things, men and gods and their kind. For, then the heart of the devotee is drawn to the glory of the Divine as manifest in the genera and species and leading types in creation, presenting in varying colours the essence, the *rasa*, of divine existence. It is an appetising food for the hungering heart, illuminating the mind with the truth of the boundless energy of the divine power and presence that express themselves with a varying stress in diverse forms and kinds and degrees in the beings and forces of the higher worlds, in the Devas and the Asuras, and in the leading types of objects and beings in the lower creation, in the known world, in sages and Siddhas, in heroes and warriors and leaders of men. Endless are the Vibhutis and all these are but an expression of a fragment of the Divine light and are there for the devotee to draw all that he needs of the Divine by a constant drawing gaze on these, the self-manifest glories of the Divine.

"I am the Self seated in the heart of all beings. I am their beginning, middle and end. I am Vishnu of the Adityas. Of the luminous bodies I am the Sun. Of the Maruts I am Marichi and I am the Moon of the Nakshatras. Of the Vedas I am the Sama Veda.

Of the senses I am the mind. Of all beings I am the intelligence. Of the Rudras I am Shankara and Kubera of the Yakshas and Rakshasas. I am Pavaka of the Vasus and Meru of the lofty peaks. Of the priests I am Brihaspati, of leaders of armies I am Skanda and of lakes I am the ocean. I am Bhrigu among the Rishis. I am Om of speech. . . . There is no end of my Vibhutis, these my divine powers. I have just named a few; know that whatever is glorious, lovely and powerful is born of a fragment of my own splendour. Ah! what more need I say? I stay pervading and upholding the whole universe with a fragment of myself. *Idam kṛtsnam jagat ekāmśena viṣṭhabhya sthitô ham.*"

*THE FORM UNIVERSAL**

Arjuna has understood the nature of the world and its Lord, His higher and lower Prakriti, His general and special mainfestations in the world, the Vibhuti and the Avatar. But he has not seen, only heard of the form of God. He desires to see Him—not the God that is immanent in the world, not the God who is the manifestation of the world from a fragment of His power, not the God that is the immutable support and Self of all creation that is mutable, but the God who in His omnipotence takes on the Form Universal with infinite variations and distinctions in kind, colour and shape, and who at the same time manifests as the Time-Spirit for their destruction; who even as their origin and end remains eternally free in their movements, Personal to the personal, Impersonal with the impersonal and yet Supra-personal to enter into personal relations with the manifold finite personality in human nature.

"I have heard in detail," says Arjuna, "all about the birth and end of beings and their greatness, but I desire to see Thy Form. If Thou thinkest I can see, then show me Thy inexhaustible Self." The Lord begins: "Behold my form in hundreds and thousands, countless in kinds and colors and shapes. Behold the Adityas, Vasus and Rudras, the Ashvins and Maruts, behold these

---

*Eleventh Chapter.

marvels; many are they, never seen before. Now and here in my body behold this universe, mobile and immobile, and see whatever thou desirest to see. But it is not possible for you to see with these thy physical eyes. I shall give thee the divine vision. With it see my divine yoga."

With the god-given sight Arjuna beholds the Form Universal; mouths and eyes are many; many are the visions of marvel and many the divine ornaments and divine weapons. His face is turned everywhere. He is marvellous and boundless, putting on divine necklaces and garments, anointed with celestial unguents. The splendour of a thousand suns blazing forth together in the sky might resemble the glory of the Divine Purusha. Here Arjuna beheld the one universe divided into many parts remaining together in the body of the God of gods. Wonder possessed him; his hair stood on end; he bowed to the Divine and spoke with his palms joined: "Oh God, in Thy form I see the gods and the orders of beings. I see Brahma seated in his lotus, the Rishis and divine Nagas I see too; I see Thee everywhere with millions of eyes and arms and breasts but I don't see the beginning or end or middle of this Thy boundless form. There is a mass of radiance everywhere. Thou art that. I behold Thee with discus and mace and club; Thou blazest forth fire and my gaze is dazzled as by the sun from all sides in the immeasurable skies. Thou art the immutable, the treasure of this universe. Inexhaustible Thou art. Thou art the guardian Spirit that protects the eternal Dharma . . . . Thou hast filled the earth, the heavens and the regions of the mid-air; the three worlds dwindle before Thy terrible manifest form..... With opened mouths Thou touchest the firmament. Seeing Thee I am quaking. My strength is gone, nor is there peace. Thy teeth resemble the devouring flames of time..... I see nothing anywhere, nor find any shelter. Thou art the refuge of the worlds. These sons of Dhritarashtra are falling into Thy gaping mouth. I see their heads crushed and ground to powder. As rivers rush into ocean these mighty men rush unto Thy yawning and flaming mouths...... Oh Lord let me know what Thou really art. I worship Thee, have mercy upon me, God Supreme. This is terrible, be pleased to reveal (the meaning of) Thy action."

The Lord says: "I am Time destroying the world. I have come to slay mankind. None of these warriors shall escape death, even without thee. Therefore stand up, fight and conquer. I have already conquered them, be thou merely the occasion, the instrument."

Arjuna says: "Oh Lord, it is fit that hosts of Siddhas bow to Thee and the whole world is joyous in Thy glory and the Titans fly in fear. Thou art the first of the gods, the most ancient, the abiding place of all life. Thou art the knower and the known and the supreme abode on high and in Thee the vast universe is spread......Prostration to Thee in front, behind and on every side. Thou art boundless in power, strong without measure and holdest the all and all are Thou Thyself.

"Oh Lord, if taking Thee for a friend I have called Thee by name as Oh Krishna, Oh Yadava, my friend, not knowing Thy greatness, if I have been careless in my love or friendship to Thee and if in jest I have been irreverent to Thee, playing and sitting, in taking rest with Thee or at meals, alone or in the company of others, Oh Lord, forgive me my error. Oh Thou incomprehensible, Thou art the father of worlds that move and stand, the adorable, the greater Guru; none is equal to Thee and none surpasses Thee. In the three worlds Thy glory is unrivalled. Therefore I bow to Thee with my body and ask of Thee, my Lord adorable, this favour: bless me. Bear with me for all my faults, as father with son, as friend with friend, as the lover with the beloved.

"I have seen what none else has seen and am content. I am riddled with fear, show me Thy usual form again. Put on Thy usual diadem; take up Thy mace and discus; be in Thy usual form."

"What you have seen this day, Arjuna, none except thyself has seen. Do not be overpowered with fear. Thou hast seen the terrible form. Cast fear away. Rejoice and see my familiar form."

"Ah Krishna, I am now calm, composed and restored to my elements. I now see Thy gentle human form."

"This form which thou hast seen cannot be seen by the highest Veda or by Tapas or by any meritorious act. Only by devotion to me alone, can one perceive me thus and know and see me in essence and enter into me."

Thus the Form Universal, *Viśvarūpa* was revealed to Arjuna by the Grace of the Divine, by which he saw for himself the great truth that God is not merely the loving, sweet, benevolent protector Vishnu, but also the impetuous, violent, terrible destroyer Rudra; and indeed it was Arjuna's vision of the terrible that was intended as the cure for his nervous shrinking, the refusal to bear the sight of blood in the battle-field.

*DEVOTION**

Such is the greatness, unspeakable and incomprehensible, of the Divine Purusha. It is true that those who by arduous disciplines retire into the unmanifest Brahman also reach the Divine; for they too regard everything with equality and rejoice in the welfare of all. But the path is difficult to reach for embodied beings. Therefore the path which is preferable and acceptable to Shri Krishna is the way of renouncing all works in Him, *sarvāṇi karmāṇi mayi sanyasya*, and of meditating upon Him in a whole-hearted yoga. . . . "Therefore place thy mind in me," the Teacher says, "enter thy reason into me, then doubtless wilt thou be in me for ever. If thou canst not fix your mind in me then practise yoga and learn to get at me. If thou art unable to do even this sadhana, do works for my sake. If even here thou art weak, take shelter in union with me...... Jnana is surely higher than practice of yoga for mental control, but meditation on me is better, renunciation of the fruit of action, *tyāga*, is still better. *Sānti* issues from *tyāga* (inner renunciation). . . . He is dear to me who is free from the excitement of joy, fear and wrath and whom the world fears not...... He is dear to me who is alike to friend and foe, fame and ill-fame, pain and pleasure, heat and cold and absolved of all attachments. He is dear to me who takes things as they come, praise and reproach, calm and content with what comes, unbound to home, steady in mind."

---

*Twelfth Chapter.

THE FIELD AND THE KNOWER OF THE FIELD

In the *thirteenth chapter* there is a running account of Prakriti and Purusha, the field and knower of the field, *kṣetra* and *kṣetrajna*. A rough analysis of the constituent elements of the embodied being and an applied knowledge of it help the soul, the Purusha, to realise his freedom from Prakriti with her modifications, in the witnessing conscious principle in him. For, it is the mixing of the two, the field and its knower, the confounding of one with the other, that brings about the confusion of imposing the character of Prakriti on that of the Purusha. Therefore, it is suggested that the human soul should move more and more through a close watchfulness over and perception of the movements of Prakriti towards the witnessing and sanctioning and controlling conscious principle, the Spirit, the Purusha. Thus far the Gīta uses the psychological method and terms of the ancient Sankhyas; but it does not stop with the many Purushas in the many bodies of the one universal Prakriti. It proceeds to the one Universal Purusha, Parama Atman, the Supreme Self who is the sole supreme knower of the field, *kṣetrajna*, in all the fields, *kṣetras*. Just as the universal Prakriti gets differentiated and brings into being many fields, embodiments, so the one Universal Spirit, Purusha, Himself undivided, *avibhakta*, becomes divided as it were, *vibhaktam iva*, into many Purushas, to control, enjoy, witness and to preside over the movement of the many embodiments of the one universal Prakriti.

Then the teacher gives an account of knowledge and the object of all knowledge. "This body, Arjuna, is the field and he that knows it is the knower of the field. But know me to be the knower of the field in all the fields; knowledge of the field and of the knower of the field, that in my view is the knowledge. I shall speak to thee briefly of the field, its attributes and modifications that are variously sung by the sages and are found in the reasoned statements and decisive words of the *Brahmasūtras*.

"The five elements, the ego, *ahankāra*, reason *buddhi*, the unmanifest, *avyakta*, the ten *indriyas* (five of sense-knowledge and five of vital functioning) and the one king of senses, the mind—these constituents of the body together with craving and aversion, pain and pleasure, stability and intelligence, constitute what is called the field including its modifications.

"Modesty, absence of pretence, non-violence, forgiveness, straightforwardness, worship of the teacher, purity, steadiness, self-control, unattachment to sensual objects, absence of egoism and a close perception of the evil of birth and death and old age and sickness; absence of attachment to and identification of oneself with son and wife and family, a constant maintaining of mental equality to desirable and undesirable occurrences, constant devotion to me by a one-pointed yoga keeping other things aloof, frequent resort to solitude and ceasing to enjoy the company of men, constant application of the knowledge of the Self, clear understanding and perception of spiritual truths—thus is summed up knowledge, *jnānam*.

"Then the *jneyam*, that which ought to be known is the supreme Brahman; beginningless is that, it is neither existence nor non-existence (as we conceive them). Yet it has hands and feet, eyes, mouths and heads. It has hearing everywhere in the world and encloses the whole world. Without senses it has sense-functionings. Unattached it holds all, enjoys the gunas from beyond them. Mobile and immobile, outside and inside of the beings, far and near is that, too subtle to be known. It is one and undivided in all beings, is divided as it were and seated in them, holds and supports them devouring and possessing them..... The light of lights, it is beyond darkness. It is at once knowledge and object of knowledge, attainable by knowledge, seated in the heart of every being, *sarvasyahṛdi viṣṭhitam*. . . .

"Prakriti and Purusha, both are beginningless, but the gunas and the modifications are born of Prakriti. Prakriti is the field forming the chain of cause and effect. Purusha is the cause of the enjoyment of pain and pleasure......"

Then there is a brief reference to the discipline by which the Purusha involved in Prakriti gains freedom from her control into the Supreme Self. This method calls upon the initiate closely to watch, witness, sanction, enjoy and uphold the movements of Prakriti. By this means the being bound to nature grows to a larger consciousness that keeps the Prakriti separate from the

Purusha so that the latter can realise the Supreme Self, Parama Atman who is the sole seer, the one knower in all the fields. . . . "For it is He that illumines the whole field, even as the sun does the entire world."

THE THREE GUṆAS*

Whoever rises above the gunas of Prakriti by first realising himself as separate from Prakriti and her works can get above to the higher nature of the Divine, *daivī prakṛti* of the Lord, and partake of His Dharma. They get *sādharmya* with the Divine; for they partake of the divine nature into which they have entered from the lower Prakriti that they have left behind.

Of the three gunas, Sattva is above the other two and nearer the higher nature, but as it forms part of the lower mechanism it is attended by the reaction of Rajas and Tamas. Therefore, it is said that all the gunas must be transcended if one is to realise freedom from the bondage of Prakriti's works and her rule in darkness. Sattva is pure and luminous but binds the being by the attachment to happiness and knowledge. (It is but a golden chain.) Rajas binds by the attachment to action. It is motion, the passionate nature, the characteristic of thirst for life. Tamas, inertia, is born of ignorance. It causes delusion to the embodied being, it binds by indolence and negligence and stupor.

"Sattva causes attachment to bliss, Rajas to motion and activity, Tamas throwing a veil over knowledge leads to error." . . . Here the teacher stresses the necessity to transcend the three gunas by the disciplines of devotion and knowledge that have been already described.

---

*Fourteenth Chapter.

THE SUPREME PERSON*

It is not difficult to understand the Gita's mention of the three Purushas, Kshara, Akshara and Uttama. For we have heard, in the earlier chapters, of God, His higher and divine Prakriti and the divine illusion cast over the lower Prakriti of the three gunas with a bounded freedom of her own, but really guided by the higher nature. We have heard of His general manifestation as world-being with distinct stresses of His power and light, the Vibhuti; of His personal and special manifestation as the Avatar; and yet all this mutable, perpetual and manifold expression abides in the immutable, eternal and unmanifest being of His own. The whole field is Prakriti, the mutable nature; the sole knower of the field is He, the Purusha. But there are the many individual embodiments in Prakriti, Kshetras, *kṣara-bhāva*, and there are many embodied beings, the mutable, Kshara Purushas. All these are in the omnipresent, immutable Self, the unmanifest being, Akshara Purusha. Both these, the mutable and the immutable, are two aspects of the sole Purusha who is not bound to the mutable nor is confined to the unmanifest immutable. He is both, because he transcends both in the sense that he is eternally free, the immutable, and the support of the mutable. He is both personal and impersonal.

He is not impersonal in the sense of being opposed

---

*Fifteenth Chapter.

to personal formulations of his consciousness and being, power and delight. He is above the personal and therefore can enter into mutable personal relations with the world and its beings and yet is not confined to them. He is the sole supreme Purusha, *uttama*, impersonal, personal and supra-personal.

Let us close the section with the two concluding verses of the chapter:

"Whoever is undeluded and knows me thus to be the Supreme Person, he the all-knowing worships me in every way of my being. I have stated this most secret Shastra. Knowing this, one becomes illumined and his work is fulfilled."

*THE DEVA AND THE ASURA**

We have seen that the three gunas reign in the lower nature in an apparently determined field and that the higher divine nature is free above. If we are absolutely bound to the rule of Prakriti and are constantly turned upon the revolving wheel of the gunas of nature, where and when is the means of deliverance from the compelling force of this insistent lower nature? Is it by a miracle that the higher divine nature intervenes and overrules the lower mechanism of body, life and mind, and shatters to pieces the bonds that bind the being imprisoned in an enclosure of the blind Prakriti? Is the divine Prakriti above passive and indifferent, and generally static, but by some caprice jumps below and intervenes? The answer of the Gita is clear. It is the divine nature that incessantly upholds from above and covertly directs the Prakriti here and develops within the lower nature itself certain qualities and powers of higher divine forces which are but translations adjusted to the limited human being given to nature. It is these qualities, *suguṇa*, generally coming under the category of Sattva that are arrayed against the forces of ignorance to give battle to them and win for the Divine the human being groping in the dark and violently dragged by the opposite qualities, *durguṇa*, coming under the category of Rajas and Tamas. These two forces of the Deva and the Asura, of the light and the darkness, properly belong

*Sixteenth Chapter.

to the higher and the lower spheres. But they are at work in the Prakriti under the garb of what we call Sattvic and good qualities, forces of the good, of the right movement; and the Rajasic and bad qualities, forces of the Evil, of the wrong movement. The Gīta calls the one the powers of the light, the riches and treasures of the Deva and the other the property and possessions of the Asura. The former work for freedom and uplift and represent in nature, in the battlefield of life itself, the conquering forces of the Divine above, directed towards the defeat of the latter ruling in the region of Ignorance below, having for their stronghold the Ego, *ahamkāra*, that poses as the presiding Self in nature. For it is the Ego that regards what is universal and divine, and does not belong to it, as created for private gain and personal profit and arrogates it to itself, rules and enjoys it and even revels in a fanciful and false personal world of its creation in the dark.

We shall make a brief reference to the qualities of the Deva and the Asura in the words of the Gīta. The riches of the Deva, the *daivī sampat*, consist of absence of fear, purity of the inner nature, a firm grasp of Jnāna and Yoga, free giving, self-restraint, study of sacred texts, austerity, sincerity, non-injury, truth, absence of anger, renunciation, serenity, absence of crookedness, compassion to living beings, absence of greed and fickleness, gentleness and humility, prowess, forbearance, steadfastness, absence of ingratitude and envy and pride.

The chief property of the Asura consists of conceit and arrogance, wrath and harshness and unwisdom. . . . The Asuric nature does not care for what is right or wrong, it has neither propriety, purity nor truth. It does not believe that the universe is established in Truth, much less in God supporting it. It is content with a natural and mechanical explanation of the birth of living beings. Its view is so limited and perverse. It is there as the enemy of Dharma and the world. . . . By this nature men are held in bondage by a thousand ties of hope, of lust and anger, striving to get by any means, power and wealth and influence for sensual enjoyment. Such a man says "I have won this to-day. I shall gain my end, mine is this wealth. This also shall be mine in future. I have destroyed my enemy. Whoever opposes me, I shall slay him. I am the master. I enjoy and am powerful and happy. I am rightly proud of my high birth. I have social status. Who is there that is equal to me? I can do *dāna* and *dharma*, give alms, offer charities and perform sacrifices."

Such is the height of stupidity, such is the web of delusion in which man is caught, addicted to the gratification of his desires and violently dragged downwards to Hell. This is the Asuric nature. . . . There is a threefold gate to Hell and that is a violent temper and desire and greed. Therefore man has to renounce these three. . . . To cure Asuric nature the Shastra is there. They who do not submit themselves to the rule of the Shastra but act prompted by desire are never happy in the end, much less do they reach the highest goal. Therefore in all matters as to what is and is not to be done, the Shastra is the guide, says the Lord.

*THE FAITH**

The doubt then occurs: suppose one gives up the Shastra but has great faith and does works as sacrifice, what is his position? Surely we cannot and in fact do not submit to every word of what goes by the name of Shastra, even when the Shastra is genuine. The Lord says: It is the faith of man that is behind all that he does. It adjusts itself according to one's nature. The very Purusha is filled with faith; of whatever faith one is that he becomes. For faith is a power of the spirit, a will in the reason that transcends it and yet possesses and guides it. Roughly this faith is threefold, Sattvic, Rajasic and Tamasic. It is purity in pure natures, passion in the passionate natures, ignorance in the dark and inert natures. . . .

In austerities, sacrifice, works, knowledge and its application, in eating and drinking and all necessary movements of life, there is this threefold work of the gunas. . . . Therefore, even when one does not conform to the rule of the Shastra, if his faith is supreme and his motive Sattvic in his activity, in his austerities, in his Karma sacrifice, in his alms-giving, if his is motive pure and disinterested, he is really spiritual and moves in a godward direction.

---

*Seventeenth Chapter.

THE FINAL WORD

The *last chapter*, the *eighteenth*, is a summary of the Gīta's conclusions. It makes a brief survey of what it has stated before and it closes with the final word. Karma is necessary and must be performed; though *tyāga* and *sannyāsa* both imply an inner renunciation of the fruit of works, the former is preferred to *sannyāsa* as the latter has come to mean outward renunciation and retirement from life as a *sine qua non* of spiritual life. Works should be done as sacrifice; for that is the law. The basis and justification of works done as a sacrifice to the Lord have been clearly expounded in the Gīta in a surpassingly appealing and practical spirit.

First Karma is done as a means of uplift, but it is also there as a free action flowing from the divine nature which the uplifted yogin, in his divine *sādharmya*, shares with the Divine.

o o o o

The path of knowledge, the enunciation of the principles of Prakriti and Purusha, the Sānkhyan discipline of separating the Purusha from Prakriti, the unmanifest Self, the immutable Brahman that is the support of all the manifest beings in it, the Supreme Person who is both the manifest and the unmanifest—these have been discussed. But there is one discipline of the Jnānayogin which the Gīta has reserved for the closing part. This discipline of Jnāna is backed by a Bhakti to the Divine Lord who has manifested the world and the beings out of Himself in an incomprehensible extension in definite and finite quantities and qualities; who yet is everywhere from the lowest to the highest, from the smallest to the biggest, in every part of the infinite gradations of this marvellous manifestation, this great cosmic miracle. The human creature does not find Him anywhere; for his perception is dazzled by the vast on every side and cannot penetrate into the intra-cosmic Spirit, into the Divine immanence; it is carried away by the illusion of quality and quantity.

Is there no means for man to discover the Divine in the world or in the beings? Is he simply to rest content with a poetic imagination holding that Nature is beauty and delight, and grand and divine or with a philosophic idea that God is omnipresent? It is a fact that man, before he proceeds to sense existence outside himself, is aware of his being and knows, however crudely it be, that he is a conscious entity clothed in mind with a body and life with which he is practically identified and in which he is apparently absorbed. If God is everywhere, as the Gita reaffirms what the Upanishads proclaim, He is in this human being also. Therefore it is necessary, natural and comparatively easier and direct to attempt to know the God who is within this human being. If God within one's own being is known and realised, He can also be realised as the omnipresent, as one within the being of others. Therefore the earnest soul can seek Him within himself. "Ishvara, the

Lord is seated in the heart of all beings, Arjuna, turning them mounted on the machine (of the gunas of nature) by His Illusion," says the Lord, and calls upon Arjuna to seek refuge in Him, *tam eva śaranam gaccha,* in every way of being, *sarvabhāvena.* "This is the knowledge I have given you," says Shri Krishna, "it is a secret greater than secrecy itself."

It is here at the close that the Gīta definitely stresses the realisation of God seated in the heart of every being. It is a great discipline, the secret of secrets, that has been transmitted by the teacher to the pupil since the forgotten age of the Vedic mystics, who speak of the *hṛd guḥā,* Heart cavity, *antaḥ samudra,* inner Ocean, inner Ākāsh. It is the Sādhana, praised and adored in the Upanishads, the sacred *daharavidyā.* The *antar hṛdaya akāśa,* the inner ether of the Heart, is said to be the central seat of the human consciousness, but it is also the abode of God, the Lord of the individual as well as the All, the Universal. He is here seated in every being with qualities, and yet without them, *nirguṇo guṇī.* To realise Him, special methods are suggested; but in practice, generally, no book can give the way to realisation. The Guru gives the method, not the written word, not necessarily the spoken word even. The Word, the real initiation, *upadeśa,* is a silent one, a power, an influence issuing from the being and consciousness of the Guru, the Jnānin, who has realised the Lord in his being, and so knows Him in other beings, in the All; and knows too that all is in the Vāsudeva, and all is Vāsudeva, *Vāsudevah sarvam iti.* Therefore, Shri Krishna says, "The Jnānins are there to initiate," *upadekṣyanti jnānam jnāninah.* For 'the Jnānin is myself," *jnānī tu ātmaiva me matam.* The Jnānin alone is the real Guru, for none else but God is the Teacher, and He revealing Himself in the Jnānin initiates the soul faithful, chosen, fit and devoted.

But this is too high a knowledge; Arjuna cannot wait till he realises the Lord in him, and cannot free himself from his compelling nature to fight the foe. Here it is given as a statement of truth, as an equipment for true knowledge. The Teacher takes care to tell Arjuna, "I have told you the supreme secret of knowledge; go, seek refuge in Him who is there in the Heart, in every way of being, *sarvabhāvena.* Reflect upon all I have stated, *vimṛṣya,* decide and do as you please, *yathecchasi tathā kuru.* But I tell you, you are my chosen friend, so dear to me and you have already asked me to decide for you. Therefore I give you this golden precept.

"Become my-minded, *manmanāh,* be my devotee, do sacrifice to me, *madyāji,* and bow to me." This wonderful line sums up the whole yoga that Shri Krishna gives to Arjuna on the battlefield. The spirit of Karmayoga, works done as a sacrifice-offering to the Lord, *madyājī,* is supported, strengthened and realised by the Jnānayoga suggested here by the term *manmanāh,* and is actuated by the spirit of devotion and love to the Divine, *mad-bhaktah,* culminating in an entire surrender to the Divine. This leads to the crowning verse: "Abandon all Dharmas, seek sole refuge in me; grieve not, I will deliver thee irom sins."

This is the final word of the Lord, the well-known Mantra of Prapatti, the great path of surrender, the highest term of Bhakti. This then is the Gospel of the Gita, that the man of enlightened mind and purified understanding realises the Divine in knowledge and consciousness, even as he of a dynamic turn and disinterested action moves about yoked (*yukta*) to Him in will and works, even as he of a devoted heart and higher emotion embraces Him in love and delight. Thus, the mind and will and heart are the natural instruments intended to develop the spiritual elements in the human being, to realise their fullness in their right relation to the Divine as much as to the human; and by any or some or all of the paths well-known or unknown to the creeds, the soul of a supreme faith that transcends reason reaches the Kingdom of God, not merely in a *post-mortem* state, but here and now, encased in a human mind in a living body, becoming a free unobstructive instrument, vessel, and manifestation of the Divine, a centre of the Supreme Consciousness, a mould of the Immortal Delight, an expression of the Supreme Will in works. This is the aspiring human soul typified by Nara, Arjuna, working out the will of the Divine, Narayana, Shri Krishna.